That Awkward Age

That Awkward Age

Roger McGough

VIKING
an imprint of
PENGUIN BOOKS

VIKING

Published by the Penguin Group
Penguin Books Ltd, 80 Strand, London WC2R ORL, England
Penguin Group (USA) Inc., 375 Hudson Street, New York, New York 10014, USA
Penguin Group (Canada), 90 Eglinton Avenue East, Suite 700, Toronto, Ontario, Canada M4P 2Y3
(a division of Pearson Penguin Canada Inc.)
Penguin Ireland, 25 St Stephen's Green, Dublin 2, Ireland (a division of Penguin Books Ltd)
Penguin Group (Australia), 250 Camberwell Road, Camberwell, Victoria 3124, Australia
(a division of Pearson Australia Group Pty Ltd)
Penguin Books India Pvt Ltd, 11 Community Centre, Panchsheel Park, New Delhi – 110 017, India
Penguin Group (NZ), 67 Apollo Drive, Rosedale, North Shore 0632, New Zealand
(a division of Pearson New Zealand Ltd)
Penguin Books (South Africa) (Pty) Ltd, 24 Sturdee Avenue,
Rosebank, Johannesburg 2196, South Africa

Penguin Books Ltd, Registered Offices: 80 Strand, London WC2R ORL, England

www.penguin.com

First published in 2009
1

Set in Monotype Dante
Typeset by Rowland Phototypesetting Ltd, Bury St Edmunds, Suffolk
Printed in Great Britain by Clays Ltd, St Ives plc

A CIP catalogue record for this book is available from the British Library

ISBN: 978-0-670-91822-5

SE208931

www.greenpenguin.co.uk

Penguin Books is committed to a sustainable future
for our business, our readers and our planet.
The book in your hands is made from paper
certified by the Forest Stewardship Council.

At that awkward age now between birth and death
  I think of all the outrages unperpetrated
    opportunities missed

'Here I am'
(*Melting into the Foreground*, 1986)

Contents

To Meccano

Like me you were born in Liverpool,
and after the war, as soon as you reappeared in the shops,
Dad was first in the queue for my birthday present.
The introductory box for beginners contained
perforated strips of red metal, nuts, bolts, spanner,
screwdriver, an axle and a pair of wheels. Magic.
I couldn't wait to turn you into small feats of engineering,
a miniature Golden Gate Bridge, a scale model
of the *Titanic*, a two-wheeled double-decker bus.

But there was less to you than met the eye,
and although my father would sit beside me,
boyish and enthusiastic about cobbling together
a pair of ladders, a crucifix or a luggage trolley,
little Isambard Brunel would wander off to rummage
in mother's sewing box. Sorry, Meccano.
My best times were spent as a fireman during the Blitz,
rushing fearlessly into burning buildings to rescue zips,
buckles and bra-fasteners trapped in tangled heaps of red metal.

To My Violin

I loved the very shape and feel of you.
The curved lightness of a body
lovingly carved from an Alpine spruce
in a sun-filled garden in Cremona
by Geppetto, the blind violin-maker.

I never tired of snapping open the case
and unclipping the bow, your Sancho Panza,
tightening the horse-hair and applying the rosin.
The silkiness of your neck as I slipped you under my chin.
God's in his heaven, let the music begin.

I'm sorry, violin, but it never did.
It was the lines and funny dots that kept me out.
I thought that if I concentrated really hard
and imagined the tune, then you would overhear
and amplify it, weaving melodies out of thin air.

You, after all, cost hard-earned money my parents
could ill afford. Plus the lessons after school.
But as a ragged claw scuttled across the floor
of the fingerboard, and Sancho see-sawed
sea shells on the C sharp, you lost interest.

Eventually I realised that what came between us
was music, and so we went our separate ways.
Me, to doing this, and you, laid out in a dusty cellar,
to dream of being kissed awake by a handsome prodigy.
Remembering, not a garden in Lombardy, but a factory in Taiwan.

To Poetry Please

What a daunting pleasure it has been over the years
to sit in a studio and present you to the nation @bbc.co.uk.
To celebrate poetry. Seven buxom women abreast,
staggering and sliding on the ice-bound road.
The red wheelbarrow. A boy falling from the sky.
Dappled things, borogroves and runcible spoons.
The secret ministry of frost, full moons and little Frieda.
Rainbows and the liquefaction of Julia's clothes.

To celebrate the joy of socks. Love in the back of vans,
sing the body reclining and the warming of her pearls.
The way we were and the way we will be. Growing old,
wearing purple, a joy to behold. And let us not forget
the vacuum cleaner and the Ford Cortina BS8 2LR.
More feel-good than Gielgud. Rhyme. I like that stuff.
Let us sleep now. To Poetry Please, a little momento,
some of your favourite lines stitched into a cento.

To Bedtime Stories

'How we envy the infant McGoughs tucked up in bed.
Night after night of magical word-juggling at the hands of a consummate craftsman.
How lucky they were, how grateful they must feel.'

The Signal Award

Sadly, you weren't around when I was a child.
In wartime, with blackouts and nightly bombings,
the printed word was rationed, and there was little time
for ill-fitting glass slippers and transvestite wolves.

Sadly, my own books weren't around either.
How proud Mother would have felt reading
my stories to me, as I joined in the exciting bits
and quickly learned the poems off by heart.

Because I write for children and often perform
with apparent enthusiasm in front of young audiences,
people assume I enjoyed reading to my own kids,
the bedroom aglow with lilting reassurance.

Alas, bedtime stories, I let you down. Grimm's the word.
I yawned my way through the classics. Boring swiftly
of fables and fairy tales I would leave out great chunks.
'Once upon a time they lived happily ever after. The end.'

I blame the war and the clash of opening times and bedtimes.
One eye on the smiling Thomas the Tank Engine clock,
'Gosh, is that the quality time? Goodnight, sleep tight.'
Kiss, kiss, and Daddy is down the stairs and off to the pub.

So inept was I, so famously bad, that when the kids
were still making a noise long after lights out
my wife would shout upstairs, 'Now go to sleep
or your father will come up and read some of his poems.'

We could hear the groaning as they burrowed
beneath the duvets. 'Oh no, not another night
of magical word-juggling at the hands
of a consummate craftsman.' Then silence.

To Contact Lenses

We were never really suited, were we?
A relationship that was bound to fail.
I lacked the willpower.
'Persevere, persevere,' was the opticians' mantra
Over the years, five in all.
(Four wearing glasses I seem to recall.)
Putting you in was always a problem.
Being short-sighted I could seldom hit the target
and you would slide over the cornea,
and disappear from the screen like a lost email,
unread and irretrievable.

Getting you out was even worse.
Last thing at night, I would jab an eyeball
impatiently like a doorbell, sending you into orbit
around the cosmos, before landing, I imagined,
on the dark side of the brain.
Or perhaps sliding down a nasal passage
into the trachea to end up lodged in a lung.
Remember the time I found you on the floor
of the bathroom, and thought I'd coughed you up?

The pity is we didn't meet sooner.
Who knows what heights I might have achieved
on the tennis court or the rugby field?
But by the time you appeared on the scene
the scene was an accustomed blur.
Eventually my aim improved and lenses
softened, but by then I'd given up on you.

Now my sporting days are over
and girls make fun not passes,
and though tempted by the occasional fling,
I face the fact, I'm stuck with glasses.

To Deya

I just wanted to say hello,
and to thank you for the good times
spent in your company without mentioning olive trees.
But there, I've done it.
Fallen straight into the holiday trap of making promises
that cannot be kept, of failed resolutions.

Olive trees, they're bloody everywhere.
Filling the terraces that stretch down to the sea
from the garden in which I sit writing a poem
(that seems, against my will and better judgement,
to be about olive trees).

When the moon is full, their leathery, silver leaves
fall to the ground, curl up and become cicadas.
Their trunks so rough and gnarled
that lovers cannot carve their names into them.
Even Robert Graves, whose house overlooks
the terraces, forswore the knife for the pen.

But thank you Deya
for putting on a good show year after year.
Swimming down at the cala, music at Sa Fonda,
vino de casa, grilled squid and tumbet.
And there was something else . . . Something interesting . . .

But it's too hot to think,
sitting here in the garden looking at an olive tree
that has become a poem about an olive tree
that looks like another poem, and yet another,
filling the pages that stretch down to the sea.

To Advice Given to Aspiring Writers

You mean well, let's concede that from the start.
Only the paranoid would point a pilgrimage of lemmings
towards the cliff edge in the name of art.

Given freely, your intentions are the best,
but poured from a great height, you evaporate
and your effectiveness is rarely put to the test.

To avoid appearing venerable and dogmatic,
the friendly and thoughtful, even playful approach
is preferred, which in itself is problematic.

Knowing there are few short cuts, no easy answers,
you trot out the usual: *Read, read, read.*
Avoid vanity presses. Don't expect huge advances.

My advice to you, Advice, is speak your mind,
brutal honesty preventing a lifetime's rejection.
(Except of course to children, that would be unkind.)

Imagination? Dear me, no. Talent? Not a lot.
Abandon your dreams. Although your heart
is in the right place, your words alas, are not.

To Airplanes

You have never let me down yet.
(Well, you have actually, many times,
although not in a screaming, texting-loved-ones,
fireball-crashing-to-earth kind of way.)

The trick you often play is to wind me up
a few days before I'm due to take a flight.
One of you will crash, often soon after take-off,
although mountainsides and mid-air explosions

over the Atlantic make for scarier news stories.
And of course, it's never your fault.
Blame the weather, or human error, it's
air traffic control, ice on the runway, terrorists.

Our adventures would fill a poet's log.
The night you took off from Bratislava during a blizzard,
my feeble protests lost in translation. Hailstones
battering the windows like demented seagulls.

As you zigzagged through the Tatra mountains
(my publisher crouched under her seat with a bottle
of slivovitz), the pilot tannoyed in a Slovakian falsetto.
'What's he saying?' I yelled. 'What's he saying?'

'He's praying,' she whimpered. 'He's praying.'
But despite the helter-skelter buffetting,
the erratic aerobatics, turbulence and flatulence,
you bobsleighed safely along the runway at Košice.

You are truly a miracle. We board you time after time,
innocent as children. Watch the crew miming
the blowing of whistles and the inflating of life jackets,
and three Hail Marys later we are a thousand feet above the earth

and climbing, climbing, climbing, climbing, climbing

To Writer's Block

I will write a poem . . .

when I've had another drink
when a loved one dies
when it stops raining
when the threatening letters arrive
when that filling is replaced
when my wife leaves me

Not as something blocking the drain
a foreign object lodged in a U-bend of the brain
But as an executioner's block
that's how I have always imagined you.

Bereft of ideas I am blindfolded
and led by the gentle hand of a Muse
up on to the blood-blackened scaffold,
where I am forced to kneel among the straw.

I lower my neck into the splintered mezzaluna
and as the crowd jeers impatiently
intone the mantra of lame excuses
in the hope that inspiration might come . . .

when I find the right pen
when the cheque is in the post
when the kids leave home
when the alcohol kicks in
when the moon rises like a something or other
when I stop worrying about . . .

Amazingly, all these things happen at once.
An unbelievable coincidence! I reach for the right pen.
A reassuring hush . . . Startled suddenly
by a swishing sound, the rush of cold air.

To Haiku

I could count your syll-
ables, but never managed
to speak your language

To My Old Addresses

You were a rugged rock, my first address,
round which the ragged rascals ran.
The sea shore on which Sally sells sea shells.
Eleven Ruthven Road, Litherland, Liverpool.

A minefield of fricatives to stumble across.
What oral gymnastics were required
to avoid the tripwire of those v's and th's.
Would a speech defect have rendered me homeless?

Eventually you bit the dust to make way for a flyover,
so this won't be in the post. But thanks anyway
for being there during my teenage years
when I needed somewhere to go home to.

6 Huskisson Street. Too many s's, too many stairs
but a fine view of the sea shore and Sally selling herself.
In the kitchen, a grumpy parrot moulted a muted rainbow
of feathers. Occasionally a Beatle dropped by.

Windermere House, Windermere Terrace.
Now we've moved up a couple of rungs
and thanks to a flurry of songs, an address
to impress with a title instead of a number.

Your days of gracious living were long over
by the time I could afford to move into you,
but the posh ghosts who passed me on the stair
with their cut-glass moaning, drove me to despair.

Up sticks, rub them together and head for the Smoke,
the inevitable and treacherous defection south.
A midnight flit to a rented flat on the Fulham Road,
a base camp set up for the ascent on Notting Hill.

70 Portobello Road. O those open vowels
O those open mouths on the overdraft
O the Carnival that kept us prisoner
O the house-sitting poet who made off with the silver.

My parents had only two addresses.
Born in a street, they died in a road
a short walk up the hill. I had fourteen,
not counting pit stops and hitching posts.

So thank you addresses both past and present,
including those I'm in no hurry to meet.
Like *Journey's End, The Garden of Rest,*
Requiescat in Pacem Street.

To Macca's Trousers

You were part of a suit that Paul handed down to his brother.
High-buttoned, Italian style with velvet collar
circa *Please Please Me*.
The jacket fitted but you were too short in the leg
so Michael passed you on to me.
On Saturday night we went to the disco
and although we looked good on the dance floor
it didn't seem right. Greater things you were meant for.
So I hung you in the wardrobe and awaited the call.
'Hello mate, can I have me trousers back? It's Paul.'

One day while clearing out the attic I came across
a suitcase filled with clothes I'd kept from the Sixties.
And there you were. But not as I'd left you.
Ignoring the floral shirts, flares and velvet jacket,
moths had been drawn to the flame of your DNA.
Holes like cigarette burns peppered the crotch
putting paid to any dreams you might have had
of making a comeback. No Cavern,
no Shea Stadium, no Carnegie Hall.
'Hello mate, can I have me trousers back? It's Paul.'

Beyond repair, I took you to the local charity shop.
But in the manageress I met my nemesis.
Unimpressed by my story and scornful of your provenance
She sneered me off the premises.
Not for you the shame of eBay, so mounted and framed
I loaned you to the Tate, where between Hockney and Blake
you hang, as Beatle fans in silent homage file past.
In the spotlight at last, enshrined upon a wall.
'Hello mate, can I have me trousers back? It's Paul.'

To Larry David

Dear Mr David, or may I call you Larry?
We have never met as far as I know
but I have seen you several times on television.
Curb Your Enthusiasm I found comic
and embarrassing in equal measure.
Congratulations.

The point is, that people, total strangers
keep telling me that I look like you
which I completely fail to understand.
You're Jewish for a start, whereas I am
Liverpool Irish, and despite the balding heads
and spectacles I can see no resemblance.

Besides you look older than me
and I believe the photograph enclosed,
although admittedly taken some years ago,
will prove my point. On the plus side
I am pleased to resemble someone
who is apparently rich and famous.

Finally, can I assure you that total strangers
will not buttonhole you in California
saying that you look like me, which although
a sad reflection on my career is meant
as a compliment. (And if it's not too much trouble
could you please return the signed photograph?)

To Mistaken Identity

The wonder is you didn't catch me out more often.
For years I pretended to be one of those who claim
to be good at faces but terrible at names,
when in fact I'm good at neither. Needless to say,
once you'd cottoned on you reeled me in.

Kurt Vonnegut is standing beside me
in the baggage collection hall at JFK.
It's the moustache that hoodwinks.
The one that has silvered with the years
on back covers of some of my favourite books.

Urged on by you, I tap him on the shoulder.
'Excuse me, it is Kurt Vonnegut, isn't it?'
Stiffening, he turns, weighs me up and relaxes.
'Mr Vonnegut may be around here someplace
but you're not talking to him.'

I mumble my apologies and rush to the carousel
where I am tempted to grab the nearest suitcase
and head for the exit. Then I see them trundle past
on the rubber autobahn, four boxes of books marked
'Jakov Lind, c/o Chelsea Hotel, West 23rd St, New York'.

* * *

It was at the Chelsea where I was staying ten years earlier,
that I first met Jakov, an Austrian Jew
who had befriended you more than once in order to survive.
Taking pity on a fellow writer miles from home
he invited me to a party in his suite on the top floor.

They were all there: Günter Grass, Mark Twain,
Thomas Hardy, Albert Einstein, Dostoevsky,
Baden-Powell, Bismarck, Joseph Stalin,
Frank Zappa, Zapata and Zorba the Greek.
Not to mention a walrus in the bathroom.

   ★   ★   ★

Eventually I did get to meet Kurt Vonnegut,
but only briefly, at the Queen's Hotel, Cheltenham,
where he was reading at the Festival in 1999.
In the lift, I told him about the embarrassing incident
of mistaken identity all those years before.

'So it goes,' he shrugged. 'So it goes.'
When the lift stopped at the ground floor
he nodded and said, 'Nice to meet you, Larry.'
Then we got out and went our separate ways.
At least, I think it was Kurt Vonnegut.

To Absence

When she goes away, you move in.
Unwelcome house guest who takes over.
Removing the invisible dust covers
from the furniture, filling the fridge with stale food,
leaving empty beer cans lying around, wet towels
on the floor. Hiding keys and credit cards.

Creating a vacuum into which everything
is sucked. Imagination, ambition, energy.
Everything except the garbage. Day succeeds
day like a stifled yawn. The calm before the lull.
You do not make the heart grow fonder
but squeeze it like an anaconda.

When she comes home, you move out.
Ousted, the lull becomes a disinfected whirlwind
that blows through the house. The anaconda
is stunned and slung, along with the gasping cans
and the fridge's entrails. Order restored.
Good riddance, absence. I'm missing you already.

To Wisdom Teeth

What a fabulous quartet you were.
The Amadeus, the Beatles.
Matthew, Mark, Luke and John
blessing the food I chewed upon.

Four-square you stood, rock steady.
Never close but always in perfect harmony.
Last to arrive I thought you'd be in for the duration
but there was a fallout, and one by one you quit.

Sometimes I take out the Tooth Fairy bags
from my desk, and fingering the bone-beads
like a rosary, meditate upon a future without teeth.
Then to cheer myself up, practise gurning.

O wisdom, now that you're gone
my mouth has grown foolish, my cheeks they have sunk.
I am become gobsmacked and ghoulish
like an Edvard Munch.

To Religion

Thank you, Religion, for helping me believe
that I am living a charmed life.
Touch wood, no disasters so far. I've

more friends than foes, four children and a wife
who is always at the heart of things.
Pay my dues and chance a prayer to keep them safe.

In times of despair an alarm bell rings
and I wonder if perhaps it's all a con.
But then somewhere within, a small voice sings.

Mumbo jumbo? Before I can tell, it's gone.
Brainwashed? You're in my DNA? We've
no idea. Against the odds we soldier on.

People cleverer than me think I'm naive,
that God is dead. That when it ends, it ends.
But thank you, Religion, for helping me believe.

To Temptation

You still drop by from time to time
but less often than you used to. In my teens
we were inseparable. You at my shoulder
urging me to take chances, to be bolder.
Life's too short, you'd say, take what you can.

But whenever ye rosebuds were ripe for the gathering
a still small voice would put a stop to my slathering.
That spoilsport *Conscience* would rein me in.
Your arch-rival, cool-headed and detumescent,
champion of willpower and survival.

Strictly between ourselves, I sometimes wish
I'd succumbed to your charms more often.
Certainly where sex was concerned. And pudding.
As for Captain Cautious, no sign of him for a while.
Been there, done it, thinks the battle's won.

But of course it isn't, not yet. And although
I enjoyed our little games, the occasions
of sin you arranged, what could you tempt
me with now? Anger? Despair? Suicide?
How sad we have grown. How times have changed.

To My Final Poem

You, my friend, have a lot on your plate.
Have you the gravitas? Can you bear the weight
of a life's summation?

Can you detain the fleeting muse?
With quiet courage relay the sad news
to the waiting nation?

Or are you just another patch
on the quilt? Another nervous scratch
on the poetry table?

Spare me the guilt of a commission,
a bar mitzvah or an ad for television.
Always too available.

An epithalamium for someone distantly related?
A heartfelt elegy, redrafted and updated?
A haiku sent by text?

The birthday greeting dashed off on a train?
The consolation, fleeting and vain,
that your best poem will be the next?

A nonsense verse to fill an empty page?
Something about a teapot in a cage?
The Hairbrush and the Tortoise?

Or are you unfinished? Manuscript on the floor.
Pen prised from a demented claw
frozen in rigor mortis?

Don't worry, final poem, you're not on
the last leg of a relay race carrying the baton,
the prize within your grasp.

There are no prizes, laurels turn to dust.
So let's keep it simple, you're just
my final poem, my last gasp.

Beau Geste

It was a special occasion, my father
taking me to the pictures on a Saturday night.
Just the two of us. A film that Mother
didn't care to see, *Beau Geste* in black and white.

In the crowded cinema you couldn't breathe
for cigarette smoke, but for little four-eyes' sake
Dad found a couple of seats up near the screen.
As things turned out, a big mistake.

I was too close to the sun. Its rays burned
through my lenses into the brain like a laser.
Sweat tickled in wadis down my back.
I loosened my collar and removed my blazer.

When the fort was attacked I was on the parapet,
an easy target. I cursed the Legion under my breath.
We were outnumbered, but when my rifle jammed
I stood proud and flung it at the face of death.

The next thing I remember was crawling
across that burning hell of no-man's-land,
parched and delirious. Then I recognized
my brothers and collapsed into the sand.

Choking, I gasped, 'Water . . . Water . . .
Sorry, Beau, Digby, John, I can't go on, it's no use.'
'What's that, son?' came a familiar voice.
'Hang on until the interval, we'll get some juice.'

I shook my head. Was it a mirage? A miracle?
An usherette clothed all in white as in a dream
was standing in a spotlight among the dunes
with a tray of cold drinks and Wall's ice cream.

We never saw the end, and walking home, Dad
more embarrassed than annoyed, shook his head.
'You shouldn't let your imagination run away with you.
Not a word to anybody, and go straight to bed.'

It was only a film after all, so I did as I was told.
Still blushing with shame, I could hardly refuse.
Although the first thing I did was go into the yard
and shake out the sand from my shoes.

'Street Urchins'
Henri Cartier-Bresson

In the foreground, two boys with dirty faces
snub-nosed and unwashed,
are grinning wildly as they hug each other.

One is bare-footed, his elder brother
wears oversized boots without laces.
Both in ragged matching jumpers.

It is a sunny day, but cold.
A lamp post leans a heavy shadow
diagonally across the pavement.

In the background, the mother
pushing the large hooded pram
is muffled in headscarf and winter coat.

In black and white, the photograph
could have been taken in any street
in any industrial town not long after the war.

*　*　*

Fade in colour and movement.
The town in fact is Liverpool,
a September morning down by the docks.

After telling the Frenchman to fuck off
the boys, still laughing,
race each other down the cobbled street,

cross a bomb site and turn
into a jigger that runs between
the backs of terraced houses.

A seven-year-old boy,
unsure of his surroundings,
is taking a short cut home from school.

The boy in boots picks up half a brick,
his brother, a jagged piece of roof slate.
They close in on the stranger.

I give them all I have
A thripenny bit and a brand new pencil.
Fade out colour and movement.

Press *Save*

As I write this, a bonfire is being lit in the garden next door,
while above, planes filled with strangers I will never meet
are flying to places I will never visit. Tonight is Guy Fawkes night,
and rockets fail in glorious technicolour on their journey to the moon
I am wearied of writing elegies for friends who have gone too soon.

News of a sudden death pulls the earth from under us.
Unprepared, we are crushed and bewildered.
But when dying is a slow and painful inevitability
we look on helplessly and hope for miracles.
We either choke on prayer, or rage and refuse
to imagine a future without them.

I am wearied of writing elegies, it seems unfair.
And this is one I thought I'd never have to write.
Midnight now, and still a smell of sulphur in the air.
The bonfire has been put out, and for a few hours at least,
the sky, free of planes, can settle down for the night.
Press *Save*. Drain glass. Switch off light.

Eternal Rest
(A prayer for those who died before they grew old)

'Eternal Rest grant unto them, O Lord,
And let Perpetual Light shine upon them.
May they rest in Peace. Amen.'

O Lord, on second thoughts
postpone the Peace and Rest
and grant unto them an Eternal Good Time.

Young enough to party, what they like best
is a crowded dance floor,
friendly bar staff, and the patron saint of bouncers,
Saint Peter on the door.

So Lord, let thy will be done.
Turn up the volume, dim the Perpetual Light,
and let them have fun. Amen.

Carpe Diem

On reaching sixty, I decided
to live every day as if it were my last.
But it didn't last.

After three days of lying in bed
in a darkened room, I tore off the oxygen mask,
opened the curtains and sacked the nurse.

There was more to life, surely,
than worrying about when it would end.
And how. The secret was Carpe Diem.

So out I went to seize the day.
To catch it unawares and hug it.
To bathe in its light, to enjoy every minute.

But the day kept me at arm's length.
Didn't want to be touched
Bobbed and weaved until it dwindled away.

At 1 a.m. I ended up in the bar of the *Carpe Diem*
drunk and counting the cost. Another day wasted.
Another chance lost.

Then who should walk in, looking the worse for wear
but the nurse. We hugged then staggered back home.
She drew the curtains. We climbed into bed.

I Am Not Sleeping

I don't want any of that
'We're gathered here today
to celebrate his life, not mourn his passing.'
Oh yes you are. Get one thing straight,
you're not here to celebrate
but to mourn until it hurts.

I want wailing and gnashing of teeth.
I want sobs, and I want them
uncontrollable. I want women
flinging themselves on the coffin
and I want them inconsolable.

Don't dwell on my past but on your future.
For what you see is what you'll be
and sooner than you think.
So get weeping. Fill yourselves with dread.
For I am not sleeping. I am dead.

A Fine Romance

Excuse me, darling, in advance
for the slow, macabre dance
I may one day lead you into.

Holding you too tight for comfort
and whispering endearments,
if I should call you by another's name,
a lover's perhaps, from years ago,
don't be startled. It's just a slip
of the moonlight.

And when the music grows louder
and the dance goes faster,
and losing my balance, I stumble,
words spinning off in all directions,
don't be embarrassed. It's just a slip
of the darkness.

For when the blizzard rages
and snow settles on words,
their sense becomes frozen.
Language hallucinates. Listen,
that's me out there, howling
at the Scrabble board.

Should I fail to recognize you,
curse, complain, step on your toes,
forgive me, I didn't mean to.
For this is a fine romance,
despite the slow, macabre dance
I may one day lead you into.

Queue Music

At a bus stop on Princes Road
two people, unaware
that there is a bus strike,
form an orderly queue.

September 1977
and a lovely evening for a walk.
The people in the queue grow restless.
Begin to talk.

Time passes, but not buses.
Eventually the queue, dying of thirst,
sets off down the road
leaving the bus stop to its own devices.

In the corner of a pub
three empty bus shelters away
the queue is sitting at a table
drinking and chatting.

At closing time
(early in those far-off days)
the queue has decided
to form an orderly life together.

Promises are made
as hand in hand
it walks out into the night.
Cue music and fade.

Love in the Launderette

Two of a kind, we have so much in common
I thought, as I cycled past her on the Common

Our bags were stuffed with soiled belongings.
Was she lonely too? Filled with untold longings?

I could write a tune, a poem or a play for her
Knowing that soon I would make a play for her

Although we had met only moments ago
Once inside, I decided to give it a go

Cried: 'Let's put our clothes into the same wash!'
The look of horror told me that it wouldn't wash

'Let's save time and money. Share our washing powder.'
But she turned her back and snapped, 'Take a powder.'

She needed her own machine. To run her own cycle.
So I unloaded, and lonely, rode home on my cycle.

The Collection

He is passionate about fashion, it
is more than a career.
Unlike a cupboard he has no fear
of skeletons, in fact he is drawn to them,
loves the bones of them.

The rattle he thrills to on the catwalk
is not made by the clicking of heels.
His girls look like his boys.
Pale and cadaverous, androgynous,
thin as whipping posts.

That he has made a fortune out of
displaying in public his erotic fantasies
never ceases to please and amaze him.
After the show the gifts he bestows
are famously expensive. For it pays him.

Back home, he might open the cupboard
and reveal to a few of his favourite boys
his latest collection. Children's books,
torn and scorched, broken dolls and toys
found at the scene of airplane disasters.

At first they giggle, getting it wrong.
Then, sensing his mood, sigh and shed
a tear at the waste and sadness of it all.
After consoling them, he watches as they
glide down the marble staircase. Click, click, click.

Not to Mention the Reader's

Having bought my wife a new bathrobe (although
why she insists on wearing a robe in the bath
I'll never know), I proceeded to Soft Furnishings.
Soft? Stupid, more like. However, I couldn't resist
the chocolate teapot, with matching cups and saucers,
before taking the escalator to the Fourth Floor.

Lingering longer in Lingerie than was perhaps necessary
I was eventually moved on by the store detective,
whom I failed to recognize despite the steel helmet
with *Store Detective* painted on. So engrossed
was I in examining a pair of towelling tights to match
my wife's new bathrobe, I hardly felt the heavy boot.

On my way out, the lady behind the Complaints counter
called me over. And did she go on. Moan, moan, moan,
one complaint after another. 'If you don't like working here,'
I said, 'why not find another job? And before you go
maybe you could do something about those foul-mouthed
men swearing in the Menswear department.'

In search of White Goods I hitched a lift to the Basement
where I bought a linen handkerchief, a line of coke
and a stick of chalk, before popping up to Kitchenware
to buy a pop-up toaster. By the time I got home
I was sorely in need of a cup of tea and a slice of toast.
The chocolate tea set, however, proved to be a disaster.

Likewise the pop-up toaster. Whenever I switched
the thing on, it would pop up and down, up and down,
so that I couldn't get the bread in, never mind toast it.
First thing next morning I returned to the store
with my bad goods to complain, only to find that
Moaning Minnie had taken my advice and quit.

Luckily, the Store Manager was more than helpful,
and not only exchanged the toaster for a DVD set
but threw in a giant plasma screen television,
as well as a Romanian girl off the perfume counter.
I thanked my uncle, and feeling a sudden craving,
headed for the Lighting department where I lit up.

The smoke alarm brought the armed-response unit
crashing in. Pinned to the floor, I explained that it was
only a poem, rather like a child's essay which ends
'I woke up, and it was only a dream.' Failing to appreciate
the irony of this literary device they charged me
with wasting police time. Not to mention the reader's.

The Wrong Beds

Life is a hospital ward, and the beds we are put in
are the ones we don't want to be in.
We'd get better sooner if put over there by the window.
Or by the radiator, one could suffer easier there.

At night we dream of faraway places:
The Côte d'Azure, all perfume and light. Or nearer home
a cottage in the Cotswolds, a studio overlooking the sea.
The soul could be happier anywhere than where it happens to be.

Anywhere but here. We take our medicine daily,
nod politely, and grumble occasionally.
But it is out of our hands. Always the wrong place.
We didn't make our beds, but we lie in them.

The Lucky Ones

Sitting cross-legged beside the statue
of Tassoni in the Piazza della Ghirlandina,
a child is practising to be a beggar.
We wish him well.

We who sit with a cappuccino
in the Via Sant'Eufemia
at four thirty in the afternoon
awaiting the passeggiata of students.

Scuttling along platform three of the station
at Reggio Emilia, a lame spider
spins his drunken web: '*Mangiare. Mangiare?*'
His cap is empty, but we wish him well.

We who roast chestnuts, freshly gathered,
and speckle Parmigiana with vintage aceto di Modena.
We who smile at photographs of ourselves when young
while sipping grappa distilled from grapes harvested by moonlight.

We who are loyal but not faithful
who give voice to the inarticulate
who breathe life into the inanimate
who observe from a distance, all-knowing.

We who, at the touch of a key,
fill the spider's cap with fine cheese and chestnuts,
the child's bowl with gold overflowing.
Aren't we the lucky ones?

Jockeys, a Perspective

Why is it
that when walking over the Downs
on a bright winter's morning
and you see horses cantering in a fluid line across the far horizon,
the jockeys look so tiny
you feel you could stretch out your hand,
pick them up one by one
and place them gently upon the bare branches
of that silhouetted oak?

(Or, if it weren't so dangerous, dot them along the pov

And yet only an hour or so later
when they dismount and lead the horses past you
on their way to the stable yard,
they still look small?

Even smaller in some cases?

lines   that   stretch   away   into   the   distance?)

One Liner

Lost at sea. Suddenly, like an exclamation mark on the horizon, a cruise-ship!

A Real Live Poet

It begins to go wrong as soon as I enter the building
and announce myself to the school secretary.
She has never heard of me, and assuming I've come
for the job of assistant caretaker, suggests I wait
in the corridor. So I sit outside the Headmaster's office
with the day's delinquents: fourteen-year-olds twice my size
who smirk and grow spots before my very eyes.
One by one we move along. My palms are sweating now.
Will I get the chance to explain who I am and what
I'm doing here? I doubt it, at the speed at which
he's stamping out villainy. Will I get detention?
Be expelled? Worse still, will I get the job?

Luckily, I'm saved by the bell. The Head of English
arrives in time to whisk me off to the staffroom
for a quick coffee. Over a scalding beaker of Gnatscafé,
he tells me that the 6th form are great fans of my work,
and I begin to relax, seeing myself in the library
with a score of young intellectuals, bright-eyed girls
and shy young men, eager to explore the jewel-encrusted
caverns of my soul . . . However, they are all far too busy
studying English Literature to see me,
and so a visit to 4N has been arranged instead.
'They hate school and everything about it,' he enthuses,
'especially poetry, so we thought ninety minutes with you
might do the trick.'

I clap my hands, and balancing the beaker
on the end of my nose follow him down the corridor
like the tame seal I am about to become.
In the calm before the cull, the Head of English
revs up the class with tales of The Scaffold . . . Who?
Before putting on a Birmingham accent
and misquoting poems I wish I had never written
. . . and occasionally haven't.
He then leaves me to it, first locking the door behind him.

I enter the ring and throw in a poem.
A girl in the front row yawns and swallows it.
Her mate blows it out in a cherry-flavoured bubble.
They continue to chew in rhythm against me
with synchronized hostility, and my job
is to catch them off guard. On a good day I succeed,
when the poems, not me, do the talking.
Having won them over, the rest of the class is easy,
and in some cases even headphones are removed.
At the end of the reading the kids applaud.
Ask questions . . . About how much I earn,
and where I buy my shoes. The bell goes
and I walk out into the sunlight, a free man.

On Good Authority

Forgive me if I do not understand many of your poems.
In fact, any of them. For I am told on good authority
that they achieve 'the rich complexity of actuality'
and that you are a poet 'of luminous curiosity,
confident in melding myth with redemptive ambiguity'.

The fault then must surely lie with me.
For I lack the confidence and curiosity
to clamber over the wire fence
surrounding your complex actuality.

Without a torch, I would lose my way,
and in the melding myth of the compound
risk being torn to pieces by Cerberus,
or falling into the pit of redemptive ambiguity.

Forgive me.

Je est un Auto

Life, my friend, is a busy motorway
and I would much prefer
to spend it in a boulevard cafe in Montmartre
drinking vin ordinaire and discussing Sartre.

Speed, mon ami, is the curse
and it drives me to despair.
Ennui is ten times worse
but *c'est la vie* and I don't care.

And when I die, as die I must,
chassis broken, windscreen shattered,
tow me to an existential scrapyard.
And before my rust is scattered,
take for the scrapbook one final photo.
One for the road, for *je est un auto*.

Paradise Lost

'I bet I could write a poem about this'
I thought, as I tripped and fell
into the keyhole-shaped pond that lies
within the walled garden of Milton Manor

I blame the sandals, a size too large,
and I blame the apparition for waving hello
as it crossed the lawn that Sunday afternoon
within the beautiful walled garden

At that instant before the point of entry
I freeze-framed, and pictured my wife
and daughter, picnicking twenty metres away
beneath the yew tree in the walled garden

The diaphanous girls serving Pimms,
the trad jazz trio, and the cricketers,
flexing their flannels on the square
beyond the walls of Milton Manor

The guests, idling towards the Greek folly,
and settling themselves into the long grass
with peaches and chilled wine, in readiness
for the poetry reading later that afternoon

When the frame melted, the noose tightened
and I fell through a trapdoor of water lilies
into the keyhole-shaped green slime
of the pond within the haunted walled garden

And as poets recited in the shadow of the folly,
nobody heard my cries, nor came a jailer
with a key to unlock the infernal pond that lies
within the walled garden of Milton Manor.

Shearing on the Côte d'Azure

In playful homage to the summer jazz festival
a green hedge, topiarized into the shape of a grand piano,
stands on a roundabout in the old town of Vence.

Every Sunday morning before church bells
are up and ringing, a blind musician sits at the keyboard
and with a pair of garden shears, tunes it.

The Flag's Proud Boast

A flag knows what it's flying for.
At half-mast it proclaims
'I'm the only one worth dying for,
Let the rest go up in flames.'

The Poet on Fire

wearing my delmore schwartz hat
i ezra the typewriter

today I will take no prisoners
no burroughs asked, no kerouacs given

light up a corso
take another slug of bukowski

within stanzas the page
bursts into flames

In Case of Hire

In case of fire break glass
In case of glass fill with water
In case of water fetch umbrella
In case of umbrella beware of Mary Poppins

In case of Mary Poppins change channel
In case of channel board ferry
In case of ferry promenade on deck
In case of deck cut, shuffle and deal

In case of deal shake hands
In case of hands clap
In case of clap see doctor
In case of doctor put out tongue and say 'Ah'

In case of *Aaargh!* collapse and suffer breakdown
In case of breakdown abandon vehicle and call cab
In case of cab ply for hire
In case of hire break glass.

Zen and the Art of Poetry

I nock a poem in the string and draw the bow

The Zen doctrine of archery teaches
that the archer ceases to be conscious of himself
as the one who is engaged in hitting
the bullseye which confronts him

The poem is let loose

That the hitter and the hit
are not two opposing objects but are one reality
That art seeks not approval
That the archer must aim at himself

The poem appears to be on target

The aim is for the poet and the poem
to become one and the same
The poem emerges once the poet has ceased
to be conscious of himself as its creator

The bullseye winks
The poem falls short
An arrow whistles past my ear

Lost Property Office

A pair of crutches, I kid you not
Hot-water bottle, full, but no longer hot

An inflatable doll, deflating slowly
A glove discarded by a one-armed goalie

'Eat Me' dates, well past their sell-by
Sheepskin coat as worn by Del Boy

A naval sextant and a coastal chart
A whoopee cushion bursting to fart

A box filled with bras for the fuller figure
Replica handgun and curved dagger

A ventriloquist's dummy mouthing a scream
A thermos of Bailey's Irish Cream

A fiddle abandoned after the ceilidh
An Alpine horn and a ukulele

Lip gloss, laptops and a lap-dancing pole
A partial eclipse and a Black Hole

Two air-to-air missiles and a Russian tank
The Braintree branch of Barclays Bank

The Statue of Liberty and an oil slick
Umpteen umbrellas and an old walking stick

The Care Less Cat

You win at the races
You lose your keys
The cat couldn't care less

Trip over your laces
And scrape your knees
The cat just couldn't care less

You develop a cough
Your lung's got a hole in
The cat couldn't care less

Your wife runs off
Your wallet's been stolen
The cat just couldn't care less

You write off the car
The country's at war
The cat couldn't care less

You try on her bra
There's a knock at the door
The cat just couldn't care less

Your wife has come home
Not a moment too soon
The cat couldn't care less

You fly off to Rome
A second honeymoon
The cat just couldn't care less

Next day there's a break-in
It goes unreported
The cat couldn't care less

Everything's taken
But there's food and it's watered
So the cat just couldn't care less

The following night
When squatters drew up
The cat couldn't care less

Set the curtains alight
A gas main blew up
The cat just couldn't care less

You stand in the rubble
Give your wife a big hug
The cat couldn't care less

Far away from the trouble
Curled up on a rug
The cat just couldn't care less.

Mr Nightingale

Coughing and sneezing
Wishing I were dead
No angel of mercy
At the foot of my bed

Suffering I'm here
In a room cold and damp
While you're in the Crimea
Swanning round with a lamp

Comforting soldiers
Who thrill to your beauty
Your nursing skills
Your devotion to duty

O Florence it happens
Again and again
As soon as I'm poorly
You're on the next train

To some distant frontier
The far-flunger the better
Where you send a 'Get well' card
The occasional letter

O Florrie, I'm sorry
But this is my prayer:
To charge with the Light Brigade
And expire in your care.

Mr Sappho

'I'm off to Lesbos with the girls.'
'Yes, boss, shall I warm your pearls?'
We josh, as she goes upstairs to pack.
Not so much a holiday as the chance to get away
from those humdrum domestic chores.
And to be honest, to get away from me.

I'm half-joking of course, but my Sappho
has a mind of her own and can be, let's face it,
difficult. I put it down to artistic temperament,
though others base it on the company she keeps.
Those women who hang wearily about the house
lounging on couches pretending to be men.

Charades they call it. Sappho only joins in
to be polite, but they take advantage, encourage her
to ridicule me, to impersonate the way I walk.
I'm fat. So what, and if my voice is high pitched
there's no need for mimicry. But she means
no harm, on the contrary it's a form of flattery.

Call me old-fashioned, but I believe a wife
should have an interest outside the home.
Poetry is hers, and hopefully on the island
she'll compose some nice odes. About what
I've no idea. Ah, but here she is, lyre in hand,
wide-eyed and trembling with excitement.

Nervous I suppose, at the thought of the journey,
and at the prospect of not seeing her beloved
for weeks. Enough to make a grown man cry.
'Farewell my darling, remember to keep out of the sun,
and may the muses be ever at your . . .'
'Thanks, Mr Sappho. Goodbye.'

Mr of Arc

She was always a bit of a tomboy,
I knew that when we got married.
Not for her a bridal gown of white satin,
bouquet and veil, but a helmet,
an axe, and a cloak of chain mail.

Should have been a nun if you ask me,
but no convent would have her.
She was no good at taking orders,
even holy ones. And to be honest,
the hooded falcon on her wrist did her no favours.

At sixteen you came along, the voices:
Tuez les Anglais! What's the point?
Why not tell her something useful
like how to make a decent cassoulet,
or where to buy a goose that lays golden eggs?

When you told her to fight at Compiègne
I begged her to turn a deaf ear, but no,
there's too much at stake, she said.
Many a true word, as it turned out.
Wounded, captured and thrown into prison.

And where were the voices at Rouen
when she was in the dock accused of heresy?
You could have pleaded her innocence.
Instead you clammed up. Watched dumbly
as she was sentenced and burned as a witch.

But for you, she'd have stayed with me
on our farm in Domrémy and raised a family.
Lived contentedly and died in obscurity.
No martyrdom at nineteen, no celebrity.
O voices, you have so much to answer for.

Mr Blyton

We were happy, by jove.
Remember our honeymoon?
Cottage overlooking Kirrin Cove.
Bun-filled days and fizzy nights
that ended all too soon.

I blame the children. Not ours,
but Julian, Dick, Anne and George
appearing out of nowhere in search of adventure.
And you were happy to oblige,
packing them off to an island in a rowing boat.

They had a super time by all accounts,
and demanded more. Even Timmy
wagged his tail, waiting for you
to throw him another story to fetch.
Which you did. Smugglers, wasn't it?

We saw less and less of each other.
All day you spent alone on the beach
skimming words across the waves like pebbles,
before locking yourself in the study
with dog biscuits and bottles of ginger beer.

Each night in bed, I felt for your body
only to feel the felt of Noddy,
or the rough serge of PC Plod.
The fear of separation, the domestic friction.
On my knees I prayed to the God of Fiction.

May they be asphyxiated in an underground tunnel.
Run over by a ghost train. George, no longer the tomboy,
molested by Julian. Let there be gore.
Let smugglers bury them alive. The boat overturn.
Let five famous skeletons be washed up on a distant shore.

But my prayers came to naught. So, one morning
while you were building a haunted castle at your desk,
I packed a suitcase and walked out. The sound of jeering
made me turn, and there they were on the porch.
Four smoking Woodbines, one pissing against my bicycle.

Lord Godiva

I am as reasonable as the next tyrant.
The serfs who work my land want for naught.
My confessor, the Archbishop, thinks me pious
And I have been ennobled by Canute, for whom I fought.

Why then doth my Lady cause me pain?
Is she possessed by devils, is she mad?
On the first of May upon the village green
To writhe around the maypole scantily clad?

Full beautiful was she when first we met,
The wild-eyed faery's child from Camelot.
Now fully grown, throughout Mercia known
As La Belle Dame Sans Culotte.

Her prurient self-display knows no bounds.
I am derided, have become a laughing stock
And vow that before this day is o'er
Godiva's head will be upon the block.

Through the town's busy marketplace she rides
Astride a mighty stallion, naked and proud,
Her golden tresses shorn for the occasion,
Smiling and waving to the crowd.

★ ★ ★

My guards surrounded her, but in vain.
The steed galloped free, she clinging to its mane.
All the way to Camelot gave they chase
Where, into an elfin grot, she vanished without trace.

That untamed spirit, full sensuous her body,
She hath me in thrall, I dream of her daily.
As haggard, bereft and woebegone,
Alone in Coventry, I loiter palely.

Mr Mae West

Went up to see her sometime
She was always glad to see me
Or was it the gun in my pocket?

Next thing
I was being two-timed
Couldn't handle it

Went up to see her
One last time
The gun in my pocket

Shot myself where it hurts.

Monsieur Piaf

No, I don't regret anything. Not really.
Not a thing. Mind you, perhaps
Edith might have been happier
had I not forced her to sing.

And maybe three and a half was too young
to be wheeled round the streets on a barrow.
But her voice was that of a nightingale
though her legs were those of a sparrow.

Regrets? *Non!* Except perhaps
setting fire to the Moulin Rouge
after battering a money-lender
and throwing his body into the Seine.

Apart from that, I have no regrets.
Rien de tout. The bank robbery?
Possibly, and deserting her mother.
But I was an acrobat, I needed space.

Had I stayed she might have provided
for her dad in his old age. Let me share
her limelight. But no, I have no regrets.
Non, je ne regrette rien.

The After-dinner Speaker

Sitting around the table each evening
his wife and children pick nervously
at their food, dreading the sound
of the tapping of the knife against the glass,
of the rapping of the spoon upon the table,
signalling that he will rise to his feet
and upstanding, speak for forty minutes.
An hour sometimes, if the wine kicks in.

How they look forward
to those nights when he's away,
at a conference, say, of managers or teachers.
And they don't have to listen
to those boring, yawning after-dinner speeches.

Dylan the Eavesdrop

Brown's Hotel in the pretty coastal village of Laugharne
in south-west Wales is where Dylan Thomas used to drink,
and according to local legend, eavesdrop on bar-room conversations
to provide lines and characters for Under Milk Wood.
Let us imagine the snug on a cold winter's night
as the landlord greets one of his regulars . . .

'Well, if it isn't Dai the Fish. Had a good day, boyo?'

'Aye, I've been out on the sloeblack, slow, black, crow black
fishingboat-bobbing sea, and I've got a thirst like a dredger
so give me a pint of stout will you. Quiet in here tonight?'

'Aye, you can hear the houses sleeping in the streets,
in the slow deep salt and silent black, bandaged night.
That will be one shilling and fourpence.'

'I see Dylan the Eavesdrop is up to his old tricks,
pretending to be so busy writing poems he can't hear us.
Watch this. Good evening, Mr Thomas, Caitlin in London is she?'

'Yes, Dai, she'll be back home tomorrow.'

'I bet you can't wait, eh? Whacking-thighed and piping hot,
thunderbolt-brassed and barnacle-breasted,
flailing up the cockles with eyes like blowlamps
and scooping low over her lonely hotwaterbottled body.'

'That's right, Dai, yes.
Er . . . "Barnacle-breasted" – that's one word, is it?'

An Almighty Gloosh

'Beautiful railway bridge of the silv'ry Tay
Alas! I am very sorry to say
That ninety lives have been taken away
On the last Sabbath day of 1879,
Which will be remember'd for a very long time.'

Loyal McGonagall fans all on their way
To a village hall near Inveraray
Where the poet was to read the very next day.
And so enthusiastic were they, and so proud
That they recited his poems aloud
On the train, on the bridge over the River Tay.

But the rhymes were so lumpen
And the rhythm so dumpity-dumpen
That each iron girder and rafter
Shook with uncontrollable laughter
And the bridge quivered and shivered, and catastrophé
It collapsed and fell into the silv'ry Tay.

With an almighty gloosh, the train disappears
Taking with it ninety pairs of cloth ears.
Och! It must have been an awful sight
To witness in the dusky moonlight.

But luckily for Scottish literature
The poet was at home, of that I am sure.
Tucked up in bed all warm and cosy
Wi' a wee dram and a slab of Dundee cake,
And for the sake of those who perished in the silv'ry Tay
He postponed his performance until the following day.

ITZ

Whose Poetry Olympics are monster hits?
Who at the peak of Parnassus sits?
Who was born before the Blitz?
                    It's Michael Horovitz

Who shuns the glamour and the glitz?
Who wears tank tops and home-made knits?
Who writes in longhand wearing mitts?
                    It's Michael Horovitz

Who's the scourge of pseudo-lits?
Who writes those fearless literary crits?
Whose Blakean vision is as clear as Schlitz?
                    It's Michael Horovitz

Who rides the blows but never quits?
Who scooped the awards at the Poetry Brits?
Who'll be the next laureate if time permits?
                    It's Michael Horovitz

Who soars and sweeps but never flits?
Who's not afraid of Jesuits?
Who deserves a knighthood and a suite at the Ritz?
                    It's Michael Horovitz

Who's one of London's sharpest wits?
Who plays the kazoo and has us in fits?
Who's the man we love to bits?
                    It's Michael Horovitz.

Quiet Zone

With respect, this is the quiet zone.
And although when travelling on your own
it's nice to have a good old chat
with someone on the phone,
this is the quiet zone.

'*Shhhh . . . Quiet!*' say the signs
on every table, window and door.
Obviously nothing to do with mobiles,
so what do you think they're for?

A warning perhaps to brass bands
looking for a place to rehearse?
To the horde of angry soccer fans
who need to stamp and curse?
A troop of soldiers on the march?
Tramp, tramp. Or worse?
A stampede of trumpeting elephants?
A disruptive class of kids?
The entire cast of *Stomp* banging dustbin lids?
A volcano bursting to erupt?
An unexploded mine?

'*Shhhh . . . Quiet!*' With respect,
can't you read the sign?

Payback Time

O Lord, let me be a burden on my children
For long they've been a burden upon me.
May they fetch and carry, clean and scrub
   And do so cheerfully.

Let them take it in turns at putting me up.
Nice sunny rooms at the top of the stairs
With a walk-in bath and lift installed
   At great expense . . . Theirs.

Insurance against the body blows of time
Isn't that what having children's all about?
To bring them up knowing that they owe you
   And can't contract out?

What is money for but to spend on their schooling?
Designer clothes, mindless hobbies, usual stuff.
Then as soon as they're earning, off they go.
   Well, enough's enough.

It's been a blessing watching them develop,
The parental pride we felt as each one grew.
But Lord, let me be a burden on my children
   And on my children's children too.

Try This For Size

Try this for size:
Figure out or forfeit the prize

And here's the clue:
Not a red herring, but a passe-partout

In leisurely pursuit, Holmes excels
Hercule exercises those little grey cells

Crosswords have you to thank
Without them, unfulfilled and blank

Tally Ho! I'm ahead of the chase
Bring me to ground or sink without trace

Hey diddle diddle, at the end of the riddle
I'm staring you in the face.

Being Careful

If I were to attack somebody in a senseless rage
(Heaven forbid), I would be careful not to leave
bite-marks on the body, lest my dental records
led the police to effecting an immediate arrest.

If I were to pretend to be a mini-cab driver
(Having first learned to drive), cruising the streets
in the early hours, on the look out for a woman
alone, and desperate for a lift home from a club

I would be careful not to leave traces of my DNA
on her body. To wear gloves when handing over
the change, and not to sign the receipt in my own name.
I would also pretend to be foreign.

If two detectives were to call at the house,
and while we were chatting in the living-room
one asked to use the toilet, I would say no,
because he (or, she) might use the opportunity

to rummage through the drawers in the bedroom,
and find the gun. Not to mention the gloves,
balaclava, and the computer with downloads
for making dirty bombs. Private things as well.

If I were to flee the country, and settle, say,
in Deya, Mallorca, I would pretend to be an artist
whose sight was failing, hang around the bars
and cadge drinks. A rich widow might take me in.

Once the game was up I would head down to the cala
one moonlit night, and woozy on pills and vodka,
wade out to sea (first checking for jellyfish),
and lulled by stars, let the waves wash me all away.

Not a Page-turner

This poem is much of a muchness.
Betwixt and between, it jogs along
managing, just about, to pass muster.

Knowing its limitations, it avoids excess
and keeps to the middle of the road.
Appearances though, can be deceptive.

For in the middle of the road something
reflects the sunlight. A silver necklace?
Broken glass? The reader is drawn in.

A blood-stained knife thrown in panic
from the window of a stolen car.
Fingerprints all over it. Police sirens.

In the wrong poem at the wrong time
you are asked to give a statement
and later, a young man is arrested.

He is from a well-known criminal family
who are warned not to intimidate witnesses.
Unfortunately, they have your address.

Threatening phone-calls, excrement
pushed through the letter-box.
Footsteps. The car mounting the pavement.

You move to a friend's house. The move,
always on the move. Gripped by
an irrational fear of turning over the page . . .

How to Escape from Prison
(using only dental floss, a large potato,
chilli powder and a green felt-tip pen)

Rise from your bunk nice and early
because today will be your Big Day.
Remove the dental floss from its handy container
and tie one end around the bars of your cell window.
Leave the rest dangling.

Peel the potato. As you are unlikely to own
a potato peeler or a Swiss Army knife
you must bite into it and break off
little pieces. Spread the mulch around
the floor of your cell nearest to the door.

I bet you know what to do with the felt-tip?
Correct. Draw green spots all over your face,
mess up your hair, then lie down on the bed
and like plague victims do in the films,
make loud wailing noises. You hear footsteps.

Having observed you through the spyhole,
the warder, moved by your pitiful state,
will unlock the door and rush in. Whoosh.
He will slip on the peelings, fall clumsily,
and skid across the length of the floor.

While he lies helpless on his back
like a giant cockroach, throw the chilli powder
into his eyes, and during the confusion,
leap off the bed and tie the loose end
of the floss to the inside handle of the door.

Jump back on the bed and continue to wail.
But be warned, he will be really angry now,
and threatening you with terrible revenge
he will stagger to his feet and storm out,
slamming the heavy metal door behind him.

Magic! The dental floss, suddenly strengthened
and made taut, will tug the bars out of the window,
leaving enough space for you to squeeze through
and drop into the yard below where the helicopter,
engine running, is ready to whisk you off to freedom.

(Helicopter?
Oh yes, I forgot to mention the helicopter.)

One after Another

My first mistake
was to do the cooking in the nude

My second mistake
was to fry the sausages *inside* the tent

My third mistake
was to leap outside once it had caught fire

My fourth mistake
was to land on the rear end of a sheep

My fifth mistake
was to cling to her fleece as she bucked
and writhed and raced across the field

My sixth mistake
was to wave when the farmer pointed his camera

My seventh mistake
was to close my eyes as I flew over the hedge

My eighth mistake
was to crash-land on the farmer's daughter
sunbathing topless on the lawn

My ninth mistake
was to attempt mouth-to-mouth resuscitation
while trying to get her bikini-top back on

My tenth mistake
was to run deep into the magic forest
and hide until nightfall

My eleventh mistake
was to break into the cottage, eat the porridge
and fall asleep in the bed that was just right

My twelfth mistake
was not to notice Goldilocks until next morning
when her father, the police and the three bears arrived.

The Dada Christmas Catalogue

Chocolate comb

Can-of-worms opener

One bookend

Solar-powered sunbed

Abrasive partridges

Inflatable fridge

Set of nervous door handles

Overnight tea bag

Instant coffee table

Sly trombone

Pair of cheapskates

Mobile phone booth

Underwater ashtray

13-amp bath plug

Pair of socks, identical but for the colour

Another bookend

Portable suitcase

Genetic make-up bag

Demystifying spray

Packet of party-poopers

Nasal floss (unwaxed)

Contact lens adhesive

Magnetic chopsticks

Concrete poetry mixer

Non secateurs

Not a pipe

Welcome Winter

Winter's here, no doubt about it
And though there's many could do without it
I say, welcome.

Welcome, for summer's tired, it needs a rest.
We hardly noticed autumn, at best
it was a dying fall.

Welcome cooling winds and snow,
replenish the earth, make things grow,
watering can in hand.

Welcome twilight in the afternoon,
that early glimpse of star and moon
fresh and inquisitive.

Welcome fog and swirling mist,
mysterious, you get the gist,
haloed lights and muffled footsteps.

Welcome hot drinks and warm coats,
aching limbs, sore throats
and headaches, oh dear.

A bout of flu, no doubt about it.
I blame the weather, could do without it.
So dull and drab and dreary.

Writing this has made me weary.
I dream of summer and feel cheery.
Winter, you've outstayed your welcome.

A Bull in a China Shop

'How much is that jug in the window,
the one in the shape of a cow?' said a bull
in a china shop to the lady behind the counter.

Unbeknown to him it was the first day
of the January sales and the store was filled
with bargain hunters who understandably panicked.

Shelves and tables were overturned,
display cabinets sent crashing to the floor
as customers screamed and rushed for the door.

Within minutes, the bull was completely alone,
up to his fetlocks in broken bone china. Dresden.
A smoking debris of hand-painted smithereens.

A sea of spouts and porcelain sharks' fins,
of sunken gravy boats and butchered cows,
Spode question marks and headless figurines.

'I bet I get the blame for this,' snorted the bull,
as he lowered his horns, stamped his hooves,
ready to charge at the plate-glass window.

'Then again,' he reasoned, 'I'm completely innocent.'
But just in case, he slipped out of the back door,
tiptoed down the street and raced back to the farm.

Yak ad Infinitum

In Tibet there is an ancient tradition
of making sculptures of trees and flowers
using butter made from the milk of yaks.

On the night of the Great Prayer Festival
crowds gaze at the carved figures
in the flickering light of yak butter lamps.

As night passes, the butter begins to melt
and by dawn it is all over, its transience
intrinsic to the sacred nature of the event.

    ★   ★   ★

The art's most famous exponent was Renko
who, before becoming a Buddhist monk,
had gone to Paris in the nineteen twenties
to study sculpture and pursue his dream
of catching syphilis and dying in poverty.

He was soon burning the candle at both ends,
working feverishly during the day in his atelier
and drinking all night in the bars of Montmartre
with many of the leading Surrealists, including
Dali, Duchamp, Magritte and Picasso.

Eventually, tiring of debauchery and excess,
he swapped absinthe for incense,
the Moulin Rouge for the prayer wheel,
the velvet beret for the shaven head
and returned home to join a monastery.

But his artistic impulse could not be denied
and once channelled into the ancient art
of yak butter sculpture, burning genius
coupled with his passion for surrealism
earned him the title, the Salvador Dali Lama.

Not all his early pieces were entirely successful.
'The Wash Basin', for instance, clearly inspired
by Marcel Duchamp's urinal, quickly melted
into a yellow sludge once the taps were turned on
and disappeared down its own plughole.

Moreover his eight-armed Venus de Milo
based on Durga the Hindu goddess
almost had him run out of town. And the less said
about the killer shark, carved out of butter
and deep-fried in batter, the better.

His reputation was quickly restored, however,
by the sequence known as 'Yak ad Infinitum'
for which, from a massive slab of butter,
he carved a life-size model of the animal
standing noble and proud at over six foot.

Then came the stroke, or rather squeeze,
of genius. He set to work milking the sculpture
and was able to collect enough milk, which,
when churned, provided all the butter needed
to make another yak equal in size to the original.

A lesser artist might have stopped there
but not Renko. Once again it was out
with the milking stool, and he was rewarded
with enough butter to create a third animal
even more magnificent than its predecessors.

A fourth followed, then a fifth, and it seemed
as if this simple monk would go on forever
replicating buttermilk yaks. The art world
was beginning to take notice, when suddenly,
one warm summer's night, tragedy struck.

Whoever started the fire and turned his studio
into a blazing inferno, we will never know.
A superstitious monk? A jealous Dadaist ?
Perhaps a band of herdsmen, fearing a butter glut
had swooped down from the Himalayas.

A lifetime's work was destroyed, and clarified lava
buttered the surrounding hillsides and scalded
whatever lay in its path as it poured through the valley.
Over the mountains a pall of rancid, green smog
hung for months, suffocating whole herds of yak.

And Renko perished. But it is rumoured
that on the night of the Great Prayer Festival
the gaze of the crowd is drawn heavenwards
above the flickering light of the butter lamps
to a place far beyond our imaginings.

A blood-red moon, a cloudless sky,
a herd of yak stretching ad infinitum
moves slowly between the stars
before dissolving into smoke, its transience
intrinsic to the sacred memory of the event.

Acknowledgements

'The Collection' and 'Shearing on the Côte d'Azure' were originally published in *Poetry Review*. 'ITZ' was first published in *POT!* (Poetry Olympics Twenty05). 'Love in the Launderette' was commissioned for the Derbyshire Literature Festival 2006. A version of 'The Real Live Poet' appeared in *You at the Back* (Puffin), and this collection contains revised versions of 'The Wrong Beds' and 'The Dada Christmas Catalogue', both previously published. The author wishes to acknowledge the following sources: *New Addresses* by Kenneth Koch, *The World's Wife* by Carol Ann Duffy, *Unthoughts* by Les Coleman and 'In Case of Fire' by Jenny Lewis. My thanks to Tony Lacey, my editor at Viking, to Charles Walker at United Agents and to Adrian Mealing at UK Touring.